TRUE LEADERSHIP

STEPPING

UP

I0027116

FROM VALUED EMPLOYEE
TO SUPERVISOR

How the best employees
become even better managers

JIM SCHIFFLER

ISBN: 979-8-218-47660-1

To my wife, Carrie,
who has put up with my long work hours,
travel, heard nearly every story and has always
been supportive and understanding.

In loving memory of our son, Simon,
who was taken too soon and will never be forgotten.

TABLE OF CONTENTS

MESSAGE FROM THE AUTHOR

WATCH THE VIDEO:

https://jimschiffler.com/a-message-from-the-author

OVERVIEW

Have you ever thought about becoming a supervisor? What if someone handed you a book that answered your questions about what it is REALLY like to become a successful supervisor? Would you be interested?

This small book captures big ideas on what it takes to transition from a line or production worker to a successful supervisor. *Stepping Up: From Valued Employee to Supervisor* will help aspiring supervisors determine whether this career change is right for them and understand how to prepare for a leadership role. Readers will develop an understanding of the mental commitments, emotional challenges, business sense, and leadership skills required to transition from a ground-level position to a supervisory role.

Author Jim Schiffler shares wisdom acquired through his years as a successful corporate president and CEO, such as what it means to operate within a "people-first" and values-driven culture. An acclaimed and accomplished businessman with a clear sense of business intelligence, Schiffler explores the dynamic thought process of deciding to step into a supervisory role, explaining each principle plainly and providing anecdotal examples. He covers many aspects of leadership, from the nuts and bolts of practical operations to implementing the vision that makes a difference in people's lives.

1

This is one of the first books in the field that addresses this crucial yet pivotal transition point in a career when advancing from being an employee to holding a supervisory role.

Inside you will learn:

- What it means to hold a leadership position
- What it takes to transition into a leadership role
- Simple, commonsense strategies to navigate the transition
- Clear guidelines on how you will need to adjust mentally, emotionally, and behaviorally
- And finally, how to make a conscious decision about becoming a supervisor and the initial steps toward becoming one

Schiffler brings the perspective of working from the ground up and applying hard-earned wisdom to what it takes to transition into leadership and build a better workplace. His strong work ethic was ingrained from an early age and shaped by experiences as diverse as working in the family farm equipment business, delivering pizzas, operating metal machining lathes, working overnights as a security guard, and cleaning floors and bathrooms for ServiceMaster. After college graduation, he held various sales roles, including selling semi-trailers, business forms, and election equipment. He knows what it takes to work up the ranks.

Schiffler hopes to teach and inspire you to step into a leadership role and create a similar environment within your organization. The ripple effects of the people-first approach are powerful, motivating, and satisfying. In *Stepping Up: From Valued Employee to Supervisor*, he outlines clear guidance for individuals who are thinking of becoming supervisors.

Let his lessons and experience give you a head start up the supervisory ladder. This is the missing link between your current knowledge base and mindset and what you can learn to embody for your transition into a team-leader role.

CHAPTER 1

The Desire for Something More:
Understanding Your Underlying Motivations

As a successful business owner, I have seen a fire in the eyes of some of my dedicated team members – those who give their all, day after day, pushing boundaries and striving for excellence. Some of them are wondering, "Can I take that leap? Should I step up and embrace a leadership role?"

It's a question that tugs at the hearts of many, and it's the reason we're embarking on this transformative journey together. We'll explore the path that leads from being a valued worker to becoming a dynamic leader.

Welcome to a book that's not just about careers but about empowerment, growth, and reaching for new heights.

Chapter Overview

If you are reading this book, I'm guessing you are exploring a career change into leadership.

Congratulations! This is great news, especially if you are advancing for the right reasons.

Before you leap into a leadership role, you need to explore the REAL reasons you are considering becoming a supervisor so that you have a complete understanding of the motivations behind your intentions. Being honest with yourself about your underlying motivations is critical to ensuring that you can successfully evaluate whether this new role is truly right for you.

The truth is that even those with great intentions are often motivated – without even realizing it – by factors that won't ultimately lead to their happiness in the new role. When this happens, nobody wins – not you, your family, or your employer. I've seen it happen too many times. That's why I wrote this book.

Thankfully, the opposite is also true. If your motivations are genuine and aligned with a true understanding of what is required of you in the role, you'll be set up to soar, and you'll find peace and happiness along the way, even when faced with challenges (and you will be!).

CASE STUDY

From Top Sales to Team Turmoil: The Tale of Sam's Leadership Journey

Introduction: A New Beginning

Once upon a time at Gold Coast Truck, a heavy-duty truck dealership in the Midwest, a top-performing salesperson named Sam was catapulted into a managerial role due to his outstanding sales performance. He eagerly accepted a promotion from the leadership team after impressing them with his ability to sell and cultivate relationships. Sam thought to himself, "Hey, I wasn't planning on that, but I am a great salesperson, and I'll be a great manager too. How hard can it be? And think of all the money I can make!" Sam's motivations were clear: prestige, money, and the allure of an easier lifestyle.

The Early Days

Sam, armed with his sales experience, believed the transition would be seamless because he knew the job and all the people in the company.

However, reality hit hard. Eager to make a stellar impression, he invested in a new wardrobe and talked to his friends about how important he was. Yet leading a team proved more challenging than closing deals.

The once-smooth conversations with his colleagues became awkward, leaving Sam frustrated. To increase sales, he trained all the salespeople in the techniques he used over the years and expected them to utilize their newly acquired skills.

After receiving pushback from the salespeople because they felt uncomfortable using his techniques, Sam resorted to a "command and control" leadership style. He put more and more pressure on people to use his techniques. When team members resisted, more pressure was applied.

Some salespeople, who were top producers in the past, were put on "performance improvement plans" to conform to the new expectations. Many of the team members quit; others were labeled "troublemakers" and were fired. Those who remained felt disheartened and demoralized.

Isolation and Reflection

Sam began to feel isolated as his team crumbled. The realization that his approach had failed cast a shadow on his confidence. In an effort to salvage the situation, he swallowed his pride and reached out to his boss for guidance. His boss replied with, "You need to figure this out. I'm paying you big money to grow our sales numbers!" Those comments brought no value, only more pressure. Feeling like a failure, Sam struggled to understand what had gone wrong and questioned his competence as a leader.

The Turning Point

In a twist of fate, Sam's tenure with the company was abruptly cut short; he was fired. Instead of thriving and evolving within the organization, he left defeated, unaware of the real root of his failure.

Lessons Learned: A Call for True Leadership

Sam's tale underscores a critical truth: management is not leadership. In the complex landscape of today's business environment, success hinges on listening, communicating, and fostering trust within a team.

Conclusion: Nurturing Leadership in the Business Jungle

The business community craves leaders – individuals capable of envisioning and embodying a shared mission. As this book unfolds, it aims to guide aspiring leaders away from the pitfalls Sam experienced on his journey. More specifically, it is intended to arm you with the knowledge of what lies before you. The journey in this book is about helping you prepare yourself mentally and behaviorally for landing your first supervisory role. If done right, it can change your life for the better: more job satisfaction, responsibility, respect, autonomy, money, and more of the good life.

This chapter is all about helping you discern what your underlying motivations truly are to ensure that you are beginning this journey with a strong and proper foundation. If you read this chapter and ultimately decide your motivations aren't what they need to be for long-term success in a supervisory role, I commend you for being brave enough to pause and re-evaluate your motivations for wanting to make the shift. I promise, your future self will thank you.

So what are the motivations that propel individuals to become successful supervisors? And which motivations prove to be too weak or insufficient to withstand the demands of the role? Let's answer these questions.

Key Points

We'll begin with a bit of brainstorming to get us thinking about the many reasons someone may choose to transition into a supervisory role. There are a lot of reasons why people move into leadership positions. Maybe your body is stiffening up and telling you it is time to do less physical work. Maybe you are worried about getting older and not being able to keep up with the physical demands of the job. Maybe you just feel ready for more responsibility (and more pay). Or you may be frustrated with the current leadership team and its lack of compassion, organizational skills, and people skills. Hey, we've all been there, myself included.

Before we go any farther, it's time for some reflection. Take a few minutes to jot down a list of the reasons you're interested in transitioning into a supervisory role. I want you to discover your true motivations.

Start now!

_____

_____

_____

_____

_____

_____

_____

Done? How did it go? Were you able to list a few of the reasons you have for wanting to shift into a supervisory role?

Now review your list. I want you to look for any mention of the following (or similar) reasons you want to make the change:

- The department or team needs guidance, and you feel like no one else is positioned to step up and do it
- You feel like you've been in your current role too long
- You desire to be in charge at this point in your career

- You feel like it is the logical next step, and you "should" move up the ladder
- You want more recognition and accolades for your work
- You want to make more money

If you mentioned any of these reasons, I'll start by saying you're not alone. We've all had these thoughts at one point or another. That said, I'll *strongly* caution you that these reasons alone are simply not enough – not by a longshot – to make you successful in the role. Does everyone want more money? Probably. Would it be nice to be recognized more for your work? Sure.

Those aren't bad things to want. But they simply cannot be your driving or primary motivations. They can't be the headlining reasons you want to be a supervisor. At the end of the day, you'll need more stronger, intrinsic motivation to find success in the challenging role of being a supervisor.

And if, after lots of reflection, you find that you simply don't have motivations beyond these? That's OK. However, know that the supervisory role probably isn't for you – at least not at this point. Did you know that 71 percent of women and 60 percent of men don't want the responsibilities of being a supervisor? The role is unique and is certainly not for everyone.

Now I want you to go back to your list and look for mentions of the following motivations:

- You feel ready and excited by the opportunity to lead and inspire others
- You feel you've become well-versed in your craft and look forward to helping others grow
- You have the skills, mindset, or knowledge that you believe would lend to your success as a supervisor, and you'd like to test, grow, and stretch those skills as you advance in your career
- Being a supervisor aligns with your long-term goals, strengths, and values

- You are ready for a challenge and look forward to accepting feedback and learning with humility
- You enjoy building culture and have a positive outlook on your work
- You find satisfaction in guiding others and seeing them succeed

If any of these (or similar) reasons showed up on your list, that's great! These are stronger, deeper motivations for making a transition that can much more easily withstand the stresses and challenges that will come with the role. If you have at least a few of these on your list, you're already on the right path, and I'd encourage you to keep reading to further discern whether this role is right for you.

Below you'll find several probing questions and assignments designed to help you clarify your thoughts and assist in making the right decision. Feel free to journal responses to these questions or discuss them with a trusted colleague, partner, or friend.

It is difficult to put a square peg in a round hole and have it fit well. If, after you have completed the exercises, you find that advancing into a team leadership role fits you, that's great. If not, that's fine too, and great as well. You want to be a good fit for the job, and the job should be a good fit for you. The goal is simply to dig deep into your motivations and experiences to help you continue to unpack your true motivations.

Further Reflection: Is a Supervisory Role Right for Me?

1. Have you ever led a team project? What did you enjoy, or what aspects of the experience did you dislike?

Think carefully. What did you like about that project? Was it delegating a portion of the project to others on your team and watching them succeed? Or was it because you were able to solve longstanding problems and make life easier for others?

On the other hand, what did you dislike about the experience? Did you feel pressure from others, feel overwhelmed with information, or lack support? Did you grow frustrated or resentful of team members whom you felt were holding back progress on the project?

The emotions you experience are sometimes an indication of how you will perform as a supervisor. If you felt satisfied with the results and enjoyed a feeling of accomplishment, despite any roadblocks or challenges, then you may be on the right path. However, if you experienced frustration with the project, difficulty gaining support from others, or a sense of defeat, you still have some growing and learning to do before becoming a supervisor.

2. Have you ever thought about your values? Do you have long-term goals? How would becoming a supervisor support your values and long-term goals?

Values can be defined as what you stand for and what's important to you in your relationships, faith, career, and personal growth. Values are extremely difficult to change. Great managers and leaders have identified their values and refer to them as a "compass" which helps guide them in making significant decisions.

If you're not sure what you value (and that's OK – not everyone has taken the time to think about this question), then I encourage you to pause now and draft a list of the things you value in the workplace and in your life. You may list values such as fairness, justice, seeking challenges, stability, family, faith, peace, etc.

_____

_____

_____

_____

_____

Done with your list? Now you'll need to thoughtfully consider whether being a supervisor helps you live out your unique values or if it would conflict with them. If you aren't sure of the answer to that question, keep your list of values close as you continue to read. The following chapters will give you a better sense of what it truly takes to be a supervisor. And you may be better able to evaluate how your values fit into the role.

Keep in mind that when we make decisions that do not honor and possibly conflict with our values, we will struggle to find satisfaction and will often experience feelings of sadness or frustration or a lack of fulfillment.

3. What are your short- and long-term goals? What does success look like to you? Will becoming a supervisor help you achieve those goals?

Each of us has dreams and plans for our lives and careers. You can transform your daydreams into an actionable life plan with a focused list of goals. When documented and reviewed regularly, these goals will help you consciously prioritize how you spend your time and what you think about.

And when we think about things long enough, we subconsciously convince ourselves to act, and when we act and move toward our goals, amazing things happen. We achieve success!

If you haven't done so already, now is the time for you to identify your long-term goals by spending time reflecting on what you want to achieve over your lifetime in the critical areas of your life. Those areas for which you may want to come up with a list of goals might include areas like family, finances, relationships, faith, and career.

Remember, goals should be SMART to be useful. SMART stands for specific, measurable, attainable, relevant, and time-stamped. If you want to learn more about SMART goals (and I encourage you to if you aren't already familiar with them), spend some time researching them before drafting your own goals.

Do you have a list of goals written down now? If not, pause reading and jot down some early ideas around goals for your life in the short and long term.

1. _____

2. _____

3. _____

4. _____

5. _____

Next, I would encourage you to talk with several people you know who are in supervisory positions and find out what they both enjoy and dislike about their positions.

By talking to others, you will gain insightful knowledge about the advantages and disadvantages of holding a leadership position. You can then decide, based on their insights, whether or not taking on a supervisory role is best for you.

Remember: Engagement, not thought, produces clarity. If you want to discern whether this role is truly right for you, you need to put in the work, dig deep, write, brainstorm, and talk with others. Reflecting and chatting with others about this potential career move will help you find clarity.

Bottom Line

Being a supervisor isn't for everyone, and that's OK! Understanding your underlying motivations is the first step toward evaluating whether a supervisory role could be the right fit for you. To succeed in the role and experience long-term joy and fulfillment, you must ultimately have the right motivation.

Below you'll find a few final reflection exercises designed to help you determine the strength of your motivations and whether being a supervisor is right for you.

After going through these exercises, you may decide that your motivations and desires aren't what they need to be to find success in this role. Congratulations on finding clarity! You should feel incredibly proud of having figured this out before you stepped into the role. Now you can focus your energy on finding other ways of enhancing your life and continuing your pursuit of happiness within the context of your current role.

If, however, you find that becoming a supervisor still feels right for you, read on. I can't wait to take you on this journey of discovery. The sky's the limit!

Application Exercise

1. What are your short- and long-term goals? Consider setting SMART goals in the areas of your faith, family, personal goals, and professional aspirations.

_____

_____

_____

_____

_____

_____

_____

2. Considering what you know now (which may be limited until you read further – that's OK!), do you think that your skills and strengths align with the responsibilities and requirements of being a supervisor? Why or why not?

_____

_____

_____

_____

_____

_____

3. Do your values, beliefs, and goals seem to line up with this career move? Explain.

_____

_____

_____

_____

_____

_____

4. Ask two people you know who are in leadership roles, "What do you like and what do you dislike about being in a supervisory role?" What did they tell you?

_____

_____

_____

_____

_____

_____

_____

CHAPTER 2

Key Skills and Mindsets for Success: Assessing Whether You Have What It Takes

I once knew a guy named Dave, the kind of guy who always delivers a punchline, whether it's a witty comeback in a meeting or just the right meme in the office chat. He's got charisma and had a knack for lightening the mood, making him a beloved member of our team. One day, Dave told me he'd been wondering, "Do I have what it takes to climb that ladder?"

He said he had been looking around at some of his co-workers and had observed that there seemed to be some who unlocked the secret to leadership, the ones who exude confidence in even the most challenging situations. "What's their secret sauce?" he asked me, and so began his quest to decode the key skills and mindsets for success in the world of leadership. Let's talk about the skills you and Dave need to be successful supervisors.

Chapter Overview

Having the right motivation is a critical first step in becoming a good supervisor. You simply won't be successful if you don't have (or aren't willing to work to develop) some of the basic skills and mindsets that are critical for success in the role.

This chapter is all about gaining a better understanding of what it takes to be a successful supervisor and working to determine whether you have or can develop what it takes to tackle the role.

Key Points

To be a successful supervisor, you will need to have a clear understanding of the skills required. You may have already acquired some of them, but you may not even know that others are needed.

You need to be open-minded and willing to learn new things. You must also be willing to accept challenges with a positive attitude, to receive constructive criticism, and to accept feedback. In addition, you will need to learn (or continue to improve) in the areas of delegation, communication, public speaking, time management, problem solving, and building employee relationships, to name just a few! These new skills will be critical to your ability to successfully set vision, lead people, and work toward goals through your team.

As you consider the broad set of skills you will need, let's take time to dig into four of the most critical skills you will need for success:

1. the ability to communicate effectively
2. the ability to manage and support strong team performance
3. the ability to set, model, and uphold a strong departmental culture
4. the ability to train others

While the role requires countless skills, my experience has demonstrated that these are the four foundational skills required.

It is my firm belief that great leaders are developed, not born. Which means you can learn the skills necessary, although you must have the willingness to push yourself in these areas as you grow in your role.

Before we get into specifics, let's take a quick look at why these skills are needed and see whether you are up for the challenge.

Currently, you are likely a regular line or production employee, and you are responsible for yourself and your own work performance. You are on a team, and you work collaboratively with your teammates, but you are only accountable to yourself and to your supervisor.

This all changes as you move into a supervisory role. As a supervisor, you will now be responsible for your team members. You will be responsible for collaborating with other supervisors as well as with the entire management team.

A new set of skills is needed in this role because you will now be responsible for much more than you were before. You have a team and a company that are dependent on you. Your job will be to support your team, obtain what they need to meet team objectives, and help your department and company grow. This will include managing conflicts, giving feedback, and balancing competing demands. Your team members' problems become your problems.

CASE STUDY

The Transformation of Brian: Embracing Growth and Leadership Development

Introduction: A New Beginning

Once upon a time, in the vibrant shop bays of Key Automotive, a car dealership on the West Coast, Brian embarked on a journey that would redefine his career. He had heard from a few of his friends that this local company was a "great place to work." Eager and optimistic, he embraced his role as a mechanic, drawn to the promise of a workplace that felt like home.

The Early Days

On his first day, Brian was warmly welcomed into the company's fold. The leadership team didn't just introduce him to colleagues, they welcomed him into a family. In those initial moments, Brian sensed he had found not just a job but a place where he belonged, was valued, and could thrive.

Initial Impressions and Growing Ambitions

Brian's enthusiasm for his new workplace deepened. His teammates and managers were more than colleagues, they were friends. The positive atmosphere, opportunities for growth, and recognition for his contributions fueled Brian's ambition. He began envisioning a future where he could contribute beyond his role as a mechanic.

The Ascent to Leadership

Brian considered the idea of taking on a leadership role because he wanted to have a lasting impact. He saw a unique opportunity to lead by example as more than a boss – to become a mentor and to support the employees in their work. Conversations about his potential shift into leadership became open dialogues about shared goals and collective success.

Leadership in Action

The leadership transition wasn't just a change in title for Brian; it was a profound shift in perspective and understanding. With a commitment to a people-first approach, he envisioned himself leading by connecting with his team, fostering open communication, and prioritizing the growth of those around him. And it worked. Everyone around him wanted to work for him and with him, and he was soon seen as a thought leader. Doors were opening for Brian, and he was stepping through them.

Embracing Growth and Beyond

Brian's leadership journey unfolded just as he'd imagined. His dedication to continuous learning, an open-door policy, and a people-centric mindset transformed him into a source of inspiration for those under his guidance. Recognizing his exceptional leadership, the company owners invited Brian to contribute to new projects, solidifying his belief that in leadership, indeed, all is good.

So now that you have a greater understanding of why these skills are so critical, let's look in detail at those priorities.

Leadership Communication

Great leaders are great communicators. There is simply no way around it. Your communication abilities will have an impact on every aspect of your work, including how well your team will accept your ideas, how well you'll be able to build trust with them, and even how well they'll be able to do their jobs. If you struggle with communication, you simply won't achieve your full potential.

So what does great communication look like in a leadership context? At a high level, great leaders have six key skills when it comes to communication:

1. They communicate complex topics in simple, positive ways.
2. Communications are concise and focused
3. They use data and examples to support their points
4. They communicate in a timely, regular, and predictable manner
5. They are sensitive to their audience's needs and feelings
6. They utilize communication skills as a tool for building relationships.

Let's dive into each of these a bit!

Your management team and your team members will appreciate your ability to make your point and show supporting data quickly and professionally.

1. Great communicators can share a complex concept or idea in an upbeat manner while, at the same time, making it clear and simple for others' consumption. You may have a concept in your head and understand it, but others may not fully grasp it. It is crucial that all of your team members are reading from the same map and headed in the same direction.

   The only way to accomplish this feat is to be able to boil complex information down to simple key points that can be presented in a digestible way with a positive, optimistic tone.

This often requires putting yourself in the shoes of your team and thinking about how best they will be able to understand the information based on their knowledge base, background, and experience. Understanding how to do this well takes time. However, it is worth the effort to ensure that your points are communicated, received, and understood fully.

2. Great communicators are concise and focused in their communications. They work carefully to ensure that both written and verbal communication have clear key points that are shared in as few words as possible. As a new supervisor, it can be tempting to talk a lot or send long, wordy written communications. Sometimes we can wrongfully think this makes us seem more competent or important. However, the opposite is true! Wordiness and a lack of clarity in communication are often signs of an inexperienced leader.

   Once you feel confident in what you have to say, it should become easier to say it quickly and simply. If you struggle with wordiness, I encourage you to draft your written communications and talking points in advance and spend time re-reading and clarifying your message before sharing it. Your team will thank you when they receive communications that are brief, to the point, and easy to understand.

3. Great leaders use data and examples to back up their points. If you want your supervisors and your team to believe what you are saying, integrating data and examples that support your claims is critical. This does not have to be fancy or complicated (in fact, it shouldn't be). Just make sure you have real-life, current data to help paint a picture of what you are trying to share.

   In addition, it is essential that you have thorough knowledge of the company's products and processes. Without this foundation of familiarity and know-how, it will be difficult to earn respect in your new role, especially from co-workers who may have more seniority with the company or may be more expert in certain aspects of production. Your management team and team members will appreciate your ability to back up your understanding of the company in a professional way, using supporting data and examples wherever appropriate.

4. Great leaders communicate in timely, regular, and predictable ways. As many of us know from experience, there are few things worse than wondering when you'll hear from your supervisor or, on the flip side, receiving an unexpected email that throws off your entire day and seems to come from left field.

   To help make work environments predictable and stable, great leaders establish regular rhythms and schedules for most of their communications. This can look like a Monday morning status update, a longer weekly email wrap-up on Fridays, or even a newsletter to the team every month. This isn't to say that you'll never communicate in one-off ways; you will have to at times. But as much as possible, consider your ability to be disciplined, and create and stick to a communication schedule. And by all means, reply to voicemails, emails, and texts in a timely manner. The definition of timely manner is: AS FAST AS YOU CAN! At a minimum, 24 hours. If you are unable to answer a question, acknowledge the communication with a reply similar to: "I need some time to think about that." I promise your team will thank you for it!

5. Great leaders are sensitive to their audience and use communication not just to reach goals and do business but also to build relationships. At the end of the day, the way you talk with and to your people forms the foundation of your trust in them. Whether we realize it or not, we often like or dislike

– respect or don't respect – our leaders based almost entirely on how they communicate with us.

6. Great leaders always think about how their teams will receive their communications and they make an effort to communicate in a kind, sensitive, and people-first manner. More on that later!

While I hope this section provided a good overview as you think about the communication skills needed for success as a supervisor, the purpose of this chapter is not to teach you these skills in detail but rather to impress upon you the importance of being able to communicate effectively as you consider whether or not you want to step into a supervisory role.

Leadership through good communication is one of the most important supervisory skills, and if you anticipate that you might struggle in this area based on the six communication skills outlined above, seek out ways to develop those skills.

Team Performance

As a supervisor, you will be responsible for overall team performance. Yep, that means you will have to hold your team members accountable. With the help of your boss, you will set departmental goals. It is often (though not always) up to you to develop a measurement system or matrix that you can use to communicate with your team and show progress toward the team's goals. These team measurements will assist you in developing individual goals that will help each of your team members to gauge their productivity.

This continual, proactive feedback system will serve to minimize the need for uncomfortable talks with your team members about their performance by serving as a clear guide for expectations, goals, and priorities. That said, you'll still have your fair share of hard conversations, so be ready and willing to engage in those calmly and fairly.

With these evaluation systems in place, your team members will know how they measure up by looking at the matrix or measurements.

If they are unable to keep pace, these systems create an opportunity for you to initiate a "How can I help you become better at your job?" conversation. Helping your people grow will be central to your job and holding them accountable to performance standards while also doing what you can to assist them in meeting or exceeding those standards is one hallmark of a supervisor's job.

At the end of the day, everyone wants to succeed at their job. It will be up to you to help guide them on their journey to success. When your team members realize that you want to help them and invest in them (and not scold them for their shortcomings), you will begin to gain their trust. And when other colleagues see you investing time in one of their co-workers, they may also want to jump in to help. Pretty soon, you will have started a wave of positivity as everyone works together to lift one another up. This leads us to the next important topic, workplace morale or culture.

Culture

Creating a safe, inviting, and fun work environment is paramount to building a great team. It will be up to you to create this environment, which we will refer to as "departmental culture." Your culture will be unique, like you. Every group of people, including your department, is an organization that takes on the personality of its leader, which will be you. So you will determine the personality or tone of your department, which can be and should be "intentional" and not accidental or unintentional.

An intentional culture begins with you establishing behavioral guidelines and holding your team members accountable for following them. In my opinion, you want to develop a "people-first" philosophy. Without a doubt, I attribute my success to focusing on people, not numbers or spreadsheets.

By asking simple questions like, "What do you need from the company and me to be successful in your role?" I can show that – as a leader – I truly value each person who works with me as an important member of my team. Remember, as a supervisor, it's now your job to get things done with and through your team, not on your own. Communicating well includes how well the supervisor listens to the team members, and problem solving can be a team effort in many instances. And the best way for you to do that is to be a servant to each of them and get them what they need.

You must also honor your mission and values by being an example and living the behaviors you desire. When your team members witness you helping others succeed and they see you pitching in to help when they are overwhelmed, you will begin to gain their trust. And when you gain their trust, you will achieve great things!

Your values also need to align with your vision. What is vision? It is the ability to visualize how you want things to go, the process, and the final product. A team leader must have a vision and be able to share that vision with the team. Values are reflected in this vision.

Thus, culture is very important to becoming a successful supervisor. When your teammates trust you, they will want to please you and help you succeed. When they are successful in their roles, you are successful as well, and the whole department achieves success in the eyes of management.

What's your biggest responsibility? It's creating a culture where people feel safe, motivated, and trusted.

The best supervisors realize that work is not just about telling people what to do; it's about inspiring their team members to do their best and be part of something bigger. Those leaders are creating both a culture and a community within which their team members can work and thrive.

Your ultimate goal in forming a great culture is building trust between your team members and yourself. To do this, you want to create an atmosphere of open, honest communication. This means they need to know what you're thinking and you can't act like a know-it-all. You will have to be willing to admit when you don't know the answers. No shame.

You are learning new things and it's impossible to be an expert on all topics, I don't care what industry you're in. You cannot and will not be able to know all the answers all the time, so admit it. That's the definition of humility. You will begin to build a trusting and collaborative environment when your teammates see you asking others for help. You are showing them that you don't have to be perfect to succeed, and you won't be ridiculed for being wrong.

And do you know what? Sometimes your people are going to mess up. Yep, they aren't perfect, and that's OK. Sometimes life and work get messy, and the drama of your team members' personal lives negatively affects their work life. This is when you must engage a sense of compassion and help them through their challenges by lending an empathetic listening ear and reacting appropriately.

That said, it is important to have a cohesive team where everyone gets along, and when one member complains about another member, the supervisor must not pit one against the other.

The best supervisors are compassionate and approachable. You want to be that type of supervisor! When something bad happens to one of your team members, give them the grace or space to take care of their challenges. In turn, they will give you grace as well. This give-and-take is part of a healthy supervisor-team member relationship.

Creating a successful team culture includes pitching in and helping when your team is overwhelmed. There will be times when your team falls behind and is in jeopardy of missing a deadline, or they are just understaffed. That's when you take off your supervisor hat, put on your worker hat, and pitch in to get the job DONE! This simple gesture, when done at critical times, will intensify respect, loyalty, and camaraderie between you and your team.

Culture and humility are two of the many attributes of successful teams. The supervisor is intentional about building an environment in which people feel safe to mess up and where others are willing to pitch in when the chips are down. Great things happen. Your team will help you succeed, and it will look like your job is easy.

Bottom Line

To be an effective supervisor, you will need to have a clear understanding of the skills you are bringing to the table. This obviously includes what comes naturally to you but should also encompass an honest understanding of the areas in which you may struggle and will need to work with purpose to gain more knowledge or experience.

Application Exercise

1. There is a very real transition from being an employee to taking on a supervisory position. You are leaving one way of thinking behind and embracing a new way of thinking. How does this make you feel? Excited, scared, or anxious? And why?

_____

_____

_____

_____

_____

_____

_____

2. Effective communication skills will be crucial for you to master the role of supervisor. Are you willing to commit to improving your written and verbal communication skills? What steps might you take to improve these skills?

_____

_____

_____

_____

_____

_____

3. Holding others accountable for performance is one of a supervisor's responsibilities. Do you feel you can have a heartfelt, direct talk with your team members to help them perform better without intimidating them or making them feel small?

_____

_____

_____

_____

_____

_____

4. Building a strong, positive culture in your department will be crucial to your success. Why is it important and how would you begin the process?

_____

_____

_____

_____

_____

_____

_____

_____

CHAPTER 3

Changes, Changes, Changes:
The Personal and Professional Implications
of Becoming a Supervisor

When I look back over my years as a supervisor, I realize how much I learned and also how much I have changed. From personal experience, I can tell you it is a remarkable transformation. It's a shift from being the one doing the tasks to becoming the one who charts the course, empowers others, and drives the collective vision forward.

The dynamics change and so do the challenges. It is a realm of decision making, mentorship, and navigating uncharted territories. Yet amidst the unknown lies incredible growth and fulfillment for you and your team.

Chapter Overview

Are you still reading? Good for you! This means you have taken the time to honestly consider whether your natural skill sets align well with a supervisory role. And you have thought through the areas in which you may need to grow or fill gaps to become more successful, you're off to a great start!

In this chapter, we'll dig into the very real changes you can expect in your life – both professionally and personally – when you accept a supervisory role. This is some of the intangible stuff that isn't always talked about, but that can have a real impact on your enjoyment of the role. I encourage you to read this chapter carefully and discuss it with your family before proceeding with your goal of becoming a supervisor. More than a lack of skills, a lack of understanding around the changes you will experience in the role can cause major roadblocks to your success and fulfillment in the role.

Key Points

Changes in Your Professional Life

Now you will get work done through others, not through your own productivity. One of the biggest changes you must make is the way you look at the work or tasks you are responsible for completing. In the past, you were able to personally engage in an assignment and get it done, many times without the assistance of others. However, when you are a supervisor, you must start thinking differently, understanding that the majority of your work will be done through the strategic delegation of each task.

The definition of a delegate is one person acting for another. In this case, members of your team will be the ones executing the work for which you are ultimately responsible. Rather than doing most of the work yourself, your role becomes supporting and guiding the work of your team, ensuring that they have what they need to be successful and that they are held accountable for quality, timely work. The output of your team will ultimately determine how well you perform.

The shifting of work from you to others is a huge change you'll experience as a supervisor. And learning to delegate and support your team members effectively in their work will be crucial to your success.

As the leader of the team, you are responsible for ensuring regular communication and an effective, open flow of information across the department. Every morale, happiness, or engagement survey I've ever conducted with employees has identified a "lack of information" as a weakness of the organization. You may have even felt the negative effects of a lack of information or communication as an employee.

And yet, as a supervisor, you are now the one responsible for ensuring open and effective communication throughout your team. You are now the voice of management for your team, and you are the team's advocate or voice with management. You represent a critical link in the chain of communication up and down through the organization, necessitating that your communication skills (emails, calls, texts, etc.) are timely, effective, and thoughtful.

Regardless of whether you consider yourself a seasoned or novice communicator, you will need to improve. There is simply no way around this; there is always room for growth in this area. If this worries you, it shouldn't. There are lots of ways you can enhance and develop your communication skills before you accept the role and once you start your new position. That said, you must be willing to honestly evaluate your communication skills and proactively seek ways to improve and grow in this area to find success in this role.

One specific form of communication you may want to begin to consider now is public speaking. Whether the thought of speaking in front of a crowd terrifies or excites you, the reality is that you are going to have to do some public speaking as a supervisor. Many times, you will only have to address your team. However, as you gain responsibility and influence within your organization, you will be speaking in front of larger and larger groups. Becoming comfortable speaking in front of others is a learned skill, and it can become more comfortable and easier for you if it is something you are committed to practicing.

The types of public speaking you will do vary with each role, but in general you can expect that you will be sharing reports, leading training sessions, problem solving in group discussions, and encouraging your team in small group meetings. You will also be making presentations to your manager or leadership team regarding departmental goals, accomplishments, and challenges.

While public speaking can be scary for many of us, I challenge you NOT to let this prevent you from becoming a supervisor. Your fears here can be overcome with practice, education, and the support of your boss. Once you overcome your fear of speaking to groups, small or large, your confidence will soar, and you'll have a new tool in your toolbelt, enhancing your skills.

Realize that your time is no longer your own. Successful supervisors make time for their team members. They understand that guiding, coaching, and building relationships with people takes time. There is no way around it, and there is no shortcut. If you think about your favorite bosses in the past, I can almost guarantee they were people who took the time to know you – to check in, to talk, and to go out of their way to support and help you. All of this takes time, but it is critical to your success.

As a supervisor, you will find that your team's problems, worries, and needs become yours, and often their needs take priority over your to-do list. This means everyone on your team will be more productive when you master the use of your time. Often called "time management," this is the skill of maximizing your work by planning and prioritizing the use of your time into meaningful blocks. The results will reduce stress and increase output, which is a critical skill for you to hone and develop.

The relationships you have with your previous co-workers will also change. As their new supervisor, you will need to establish and maintain a new boundary to become an effective leader. For example, you should think carefully before socializing or spending extended amounts of time with any one of your employees. Other employees may misinterpret those relationships and feel you are giving them preferential treatment. This means you may have to distance yourself respectfully and carefully from current friendships, especially if those co-workers report to you.

During this transition, many supervisors and leaders experience feelings of loneliness until they form relationships with others who are on their new leadership team. This phenomenon of loneliness is real, and you must develop strategies to overcome those feelings.

Finally, you will have to develop problem-solving skills. Your reports – or people whom you supervise – are going to approach you with many challenges, and they'll look to you to either solve the problem yourself (or, more ideally, help them solve the problem). As their supervisor, you will have to brainstorm and mentor them through their problems or find additional resources and help them find solutions. Strengthening your problem-solving skills can help you become a more confident and effective leader and thought partner for them during these tough moments.

Changes in Your Personal Life

You'll work outside of typical hours. Some people think that when they become supervisors, they will work fewer hours and get more pay. It simply doesn't work that way. For example, if you have a background in production, you are likely working a regimented 40-hour work week. When stepping into a supervisory role, you should expect to work more than 40 hours per week. Plan on working a 45-hour week (at a minimum) because there are things that need to be done before or after working hours. Expect to start work early and stay late. You now have more responsibility and the buck stops with you. You may also need to be available during evenings, weekends, and holidays.

Every manager, CEO, organization, and industry has expectations. I encourage you to ask your manager about this and become fully informed about what will be expected of you before taking on a supervisory role. Once you have a clear sense of what will be required of you, have an in-depth conversation with your family about how these new hours and responsibilities will impact family time to ensure that everyone understands the expectations of your new role.

You will take on the emotions, problems, and needs of your team. The additional responsibilities of your role, plus the ownership you'll have over the roles and needs of others, will ultimately add stress to your life. As your employees struggle with frustration, challenges, and setbacks, so too will you, right there along with them. In some ways, their struggles become yours, and it can be very hard to set those burdens down at the end of the day. Great leaders learn to handle stress in creative, healthy ways. They understand what is within their control and what is not. They work intentionally to channel their energy into solving problems within their area of control rather than dwelling on things they cannot change. Experience, education, growth, mentoring, and maturity will assist in developing these skills.

It's Not All Bad!
Positive Aspects of Being a Supervisor

While there are certainly new challenges to face when you become a supervisor, there are also many benefits to becoming a supervisor. Some are monetary, but most are emotional. Often your pay will increase, which will allow you to improve your quality of life. More importantly, if you embrace your new responsibilities and implement a people-first philosophy, you will gain the respect and trust of both leadership and your team and will make a difference for the entire organization.

As you master the new skill sets we discussed earlier and achieve success, you will gain momentum in your role. You will have access to more information and the opportunity to influence decision making, along with having access to more resources. This will allow you to have greater and greater influence to make things better for your team. Your successes will build your confidence, and you will find yourself accomplishing organizational, personal, and financial goals you never imagined possible. The results will change your outlook regarding life, family, your company, and the world.

Bottom Line

When you decide to take on a supervisory role, there are very real implications for your personal and professional life. Some will feel challenging and cause some growing pains, while others will be positive, allowing you to enjoy new perks and fulfillment in your role. Before you commit to a supervisory role, make sure you (and your family) understand the real implications of your decision and are prepared with a plan to ride the waves that will inevitably come as you get accustomed to your new role.

Application Exercise

1. Do you understand the concept of delegation? What is it? Do you think you will be able to let go of the things you've done in the past and let others do them? What challenges do you anticipate experiencing regarding delegation?

_____

_____

_____

_____

_____

_____

_____

_____

_____

2. Do you feel you are a good communicator? If yes, why? What areas of communication do you feel you need help with – verbal or written? How are your email and computer skills?

_____

_____

_____

_____

_____

_____

3. Do you anticipate any challenges with your current co-workers if you are promoted? If yes, explain. Will you have to distance yourself from any of your co-workers who are currently your friends? If yes, which ones?

_____

_____

_____

_____

_____

_____

4. As a supervisor, you will be expected to work longer hours and take on more responsibility. Are you prepared to do this? What relationships will suffer and what sacrifices are you willing to make to accommodate the extra demands on your time and additional responsibilities?

_____

_____

_____

_____

_____

_____

5. Job satisfaction is one of the biggest rewards of being a supervisor, as you are in a position to make a difference in the lives of those you supervise and also in the company's success. What are your concerns? What excites you about being a supervisor?

_____

_____

_____

_____

_____

_____

_____

CHAPTER 4

Common Misconceptions: Gaining a True Understanding of the Supervisor's Role

I love watching the Olympics and I'm always caught off-guard by how easy the athletes make things look! For example, the bobsledders just push off from the top of the chute, jump in their sleds, and hurtle down the track with the team merely along for the ride. They only apply their brakes at the end and that's only to slow down. They then jump right out of the sled at the end of the ride.

Easy, right?

Same thing with downhill skiers. They just point their skis down the hill and take off, right? And don't even get me started with curling, Minnesota's number-one claim to fame! I mean, these are adults pushing a stone down a strip of ice, and other grown-ups are sweeping the ice fast and furiously with a broom, keeping just inches ahead of a gliding rock with a handle.

They make it look so easy. If we only had the courage, we could just climb into that bobsled, slap on those skis, or push that rock down the ice and win a medal.

Good supervisors are the same way. We've all seen supervisors who walk around and talk to people, looking relaxed and chill. When problems arise, they walk in and say a few words, and all is well! Is this reality? Is being a supervisor as easy as it looks?

The short answer is: of course not. Behind the scenes, being a supervisor is full of challenges; it is just that great managers don't let you see that when you interact with them. They can communicate clearly, show kindness, and think clearly, even when they are absolutely in over their heads with stress and work. Not surprisingly, this reality has led to one of the biggest misconceptions out there about being a supervisor, namely that it is easy work and anyone can do it.

Chapter Overview

"It's easy work" isn't the only common misconception about being a manager that is circulating out there in the business world. This chapter is dedicated to unpacking a few key misconceptions and misunderstandings about what it takes to be successful in this role. Ensuring that you possess a clear understanding of the role's requirements and avoiding common misconceptions can bring you closer to determining whether this path is suitable for you.

Key Points

Common Misconceptions

Misconception #1: Supervisors are responsible for everything.

This simply isn't true and thank goodness it isn't. Just as your team members are part of your team, supervisors are part of a larger management team. Companies, no matter how large or small, have an organizational structure in place to guide supervisors. There are policies and procedures in place to assist leadership and help delineate what does and doesn't fall within a supervisor's realm of responsibility. Sometimes this is well documented but often it is not.

However, your boss should be able to guide you. She or he will be a resource to help you clarify the scope of your role and your key responsibilities. Even though, at times, it may feel like everything is falling in your lap, it's critical to remember that the success of the entire company does not rest on your shoulders alone. It truly is a team responsibility, and everyone plays a part in the company's success or failure. Always remember to stay focused on your area of responsibility. When you lose focus, bad things can happen.

Misconception #2: Supervisors must make all their own decisions without support.

Again, supervisors have resources at their disposal to help them solve workplace dilemmas and make key decisions. Such resources include the leadership team, mission and vision statements, policy manuals, safety manuals, and the Human Resources Department. While those resources may be available, you may still need to ask for help in order to act as an advocate for your team and provide everyone (yourself included) with any needed support. As time passes, you will gain experience, which will give you more and more confidence in your decision-making process.

I have found that referring to the company's values, goals, and vision statements can be a good guide in decision making. However, if your company doesn't have them in place, by all means, step forward and create them for your department. You will find them valuable in leading your team. They can truly give you a roadmap and assist you in making difficult decisions. If you're making decisions that align with the company's values and mission (and hopefully your own values as well), you can trust that you will have the support of your boss and management. Your team will notice your philosophies are in alignment with the company's values, and their respect for you and trust in you will grow. Values-based leadership reaps infinite rewards, and I encourage you to read up on the topic.

Misconception #3: Being a supervisor isn't as stressful as doing hands-on work. It's a "cush" job.

I'm guessing that by reading this book, you've figured out that this statement is not true. Being a supervisor can be a stressful job. Stress will be part of your new normal. The stress will usually involve dealing with people, not doing the tasks themselves. Your team members, boss, other supervisors, suppliers, vendors, customers, and your family will come to you with problems. It will be your job to be a good listener and hear them. Then assist and support them however possible to help find solutions.

You will have to learn how to function and excel in times of stress. That said, know that dealing with stress well is a learned skill. Some ideas for dealing with stress might be:

- Take a series of deep breaths, breathing in through your nose for three seconds, holding for three seconds, and breathing out through your nose for three seconds
- Give yourself time to process things by counting to 10 before responding
- Take a walk away from the situation to collect your thoughts
- Talk to a trusted friend, peer, family member, or supervisor about the situation

You truly can get better at it with time, and most successful supervisors do. You will find that referring to your personal leadership philosophy, vision, mission, and values will remind you of what is important. This will be helpful in finding balance so you can move forward with clarity in times of stress. Once you know what to focus on, you will experience calmness and establish your priorities.

When facing stress, you have a choice: You can acknowledge the stress, work with it, and navigate through it in healthy ways, or you can push it aside and try to ignore it. Those who have not addressed their stress often create much bigger challenges for themselves and others. This can sometimes lead to lashing out at employees or family members or engaging in drinking, drug abuse, or other harmful behaviors. If you find yourself reacting poorly, ask for help and learn how to address your stress in healthy ways.

Misconception #4: You must be a natural-born leader.

Let's debunk this myth once and for all. From my years of experience, I have come to believe that the very best leaders are the ones who don't necessarily label themselves as "natural-born leaders." They're not the ones who think they have all the answers. Rather, they are the individuals who humbly embrace the concept of lifelong learning and feel they can make a difference.

The truth is no one starts a new position knowing everything. We all begin our leadership journey somewhere. Choose to become a sponge of information on leadership from sources such as books, podcasts, YouTube, and online training courses. You will begin to become more and more comfortable in your role, and eventually experience will shape you into the leader you are destined to become.

Bottom Line

Many things need to be clarified about what it takes to be a supervisor. Having a clear understanding of the role is critical to your ability to accurately assess whether this role is right for you. Before proceeding, you may want to talk with other leaders about their experiences. The more clarity you have, the closer your reality will be to your expectations, leading to higher job satisfaction and fulfillment.

Application Exercise

1. As you think about becoming a supervisor, what expectations do you have of yourself in the role? Do you think these expectations are healthy and reasonable?

_____

_____

_____

_____

_____

_____

_____

2. You are going to have to ask for help at times because you can't do it all yourself. Is asking for help hard for you and, if so, what steps can you take to overcome this?

_____

_____

_____

_____

_____

_____

_____

3. How have you handled stress in the past? Are you concerned about how you might react to stress if you experience it on a more frequent basis?

_____

_____

_____

_____

_____

_____

_____

_____

CHAPTER 5

A Day in the Life of a Supervisor: Meetings and Routines as Tools for Success

Ever wonder why managers seem to be in meetings all day long? We've all heard the joke: "Because they're too busy making decisions to get any actual work done!" While this jest brings a chuckle, it touches upon a crucial aspect of effective leadership.

Meetings and routines are the heartbeat of leadership teams, which are not just about making decisions. Leadership teams shape a company's or organization's direction, foster collaboration, and steer the ship toward success.

Chapter Overview

Congratulations on making it this far! As you continue to explore whether becoming a supervisor is right for you, you must start to get a sense of what the day-to-day life of a supervisor looks like. While each supervisor's day will ultimately look different, they all have a few things in common that form the anchors and create the rhythm for supervisory work.

In this chapter, we will explore meetings and routines as key vehicles for getting work done as well as building trust and open communication within your team and with management. As you read this chapter, I encourage you to reflect on the relevance and importance of this quote:

"If you are going to achieve excellence in big things,
you have to develop the habit in little matters."

Key Points

As I shared in the introduction, your days as a supervisor should revolve around practices that allow for effective communication with and support of your team. Here are two key components of a supervisor's day that promote the development of these important goals:

Big Idea #1: As a supervisor, your day will revolve around communication with your team, often via meetings.

This communication can take many forms, but meetings (of various kinds) are one form of face-to-face communication that will play a key role in your success. As you work to build relationships and get things done, meetings will take up much of your time. It's important for you to understand the names and purposes of the numerous meetings you may participate in or lead:

- stand-up huddles
- one-on-one meetings (often with your manager or a team member)
- monthly or quarterly team meetings
- annual meetings

Let's look a bit more closely at each of these:

Huddles

A huddle is a quick, often 10- to 15-minute meeting designed to get everyone on the team together and on the same page with the day's plans. Huddles are especially useful when you need to highlight priorities and goals for the day or share recent updates or changes to the day's plans. It is helpful to announce when someone is out sick, and the team needs to brainstorm a coverage plan. It also creates an opportunity for team members to voice any concerns or needs for the day so that they can be addressed quickly. Huddles can be a game changer in your effectiveness and agility as a team.

One-on-One Meetings with Your Team Members

Next, I encourage you to meet one-on-one monthly (or even weekly if needed) with each member of your team. These meetings provide a critical space to set and track progress toward goals, grow and develop your people, and build trusting relationships by getting to know one another on a more personal level. These meetings can be as short as 15 minutes or as long as an hour. You'll want to follow a consistent format or agenda so your team members know how to prepare and what to expect.

One-on-One Meetings with Your Manager

In addition to meeting with your team members, you will want to meet with your manager regularly. This will help keep him or her in the loop about what is going on in the department, your challenges and concerns, and any issues you are having with your team. These meetings give you and your boss a useful time for updates and communication, as well as a chance to work together to solve some of your biggest problems. It is your responsibility to make sure your boss is never in the dark about what's going on with your team. They should also provide you with support and professional development as you learn and grow in your role.

Over time, you can share with your manager your goals, aspirations, and observations, and he or she can share with you what's going on in the company from a different perspective and give you the information you need to do a good job. It's a win-win scenario.

While a fixed one-on-one meeting is ideal, that may not always be possible. Whether or not you have formal meetings with your manager, I would encourage you to find a creative, consistent way to give him or her a weekly update. That might involve a simple email or voicemail, or it could even be a stand-up meeting when you bump into one another. The point here is that you want to have a regular way to keep your manager updated and ensure you can collaborate to strengthen this important relationship.

Quarterly or Monthly Meetings

Quarterly or monthly meetings play an important role in your ability to manage your team's work. These meetings are held regularly to give you a chance to reflect on the short-term past and set short-term goals, either monthly or quarterly. These meetings are often at least an hour in length (no standing for these!) and follow a predictable structure or agenda at each meeting.

I like to begin with shout-outs or other positive recognition for individuals and teams, as appropriate. Then I move into a summary of progress toward goals over the past period (with a look at areas we struggled with as well as high points). I follow this with planning and goal-setting for the next period. These meetings are critical to providing space for your entire team to reflect on recent work and reset goals and priorities as needed. Don't skip these meetings! They are game-changers in your effectiveness.

Annual Meetings

Annual meetings are similar to monthly or quarterly meetings. However, they take into consideration the entire previous year (either a fiscal or calendar year) and then look ahead to the coming year. They provide a great opportunity to engage in some culture-enhancing or team-building activities. Great organizations invest in annual meetings to keep all team members informed and provide meaningful experiences that foster relationships, celebration, and goal-setting in ways that inspire and excite their teams. Don't forget to include food! Good things happen when people break bread together.

Big Idea #2: As a supervisor, your day will require you to engage in a set of processes or routines to ensure consistent outcomes.

Great supervisors are highly structured. They carefully plan their days to ensure that they meet various objectives on a regular schedule. Let's look at two key routines that lead to success and that support good communication with your team and management. As you read, I encourage you to reflect on how well you currently create and adhere to processes and routines, understanding that you'll need to be very skilled and consistent in this area to find success as a supervisor.

Just as in sports, the fundamentals are very important. And yet, that's what many forget. If you are going to achieve excellence in big things, you need to develop the habit in little matters.

Walkabouts

Every morning, I greet my team members in their space. In my case, that means I walk the facility and yard. This gives me the opportunity to check on things and make sure everything is in order. But most importantly, it gives me a chance to interact with my team members in their space.

I have learned over the years that nobody wants to be called into their boss' office. Just as in high school, when no one wanted to be sent to the principal's office, the common perception is that nothing good happens there.

I believe in going to my team members' space because they're comfortable in their own space. I usually share a simple greeting like, "Good morning!" or ask questions such as, "How's your family doing?"

This permits people, over time, to approach you on whatever issues are on their minds. It might be informing you of a personal victory at home or voicing their concern over a co-worker, equipment maintenance, or a personal dilemma.

Your walkabout gives your team members an opportunity to talk to you in a comfortable space – their space. This allows you both to celebrate life's wins or problem-solve life's issues. So each morning, I make sure to greet people in their environment. This simple practice has the power to transform your effectiveness and your relationships.

Starting Early and Ending Late

As a supervisor, you need to be the first to arrive and the last to go home. This is important because, if and when unplanned events happen, you are the first to know. It may be a no-call/no-show, a sick team member, an icy sidewalk, a power outage, or a rush order. You will be actively addressing the issue before your team begins their workday. This is also important because, in the end, you are accountable for your team. Arriving early will give you the extra time needed to respond to the unexpected and prepare for the day in ways that assure your team that things are under control.

Similarly, as a supervisor, you will learn that staying longer provides several benefits. It allows you to walk the floor, make sure that things are locked up, check that tools and equipment are put away, and review the day.

As you're closing up, ask yourself what went right, what went wrong, and what still needs to be addressed. Make some notes and wisely use the time to get your head around the plan for tomorrow. Time spent closing out your day will give you a fresh start on the next day.

As a supervisor, your day will focus on people. As you've learned throughout this book, your role as a supervisor is more about people than it is about tasks. Your day should be filled with meetings and other routines that enhance relationships with your team and management. This will allow you to build trust; this trust will help you through challenging times.

Bottom Line

Supervisors must find effective and consistent ways to communicate key information with their employees to improve effectiveness, support culture, and grow trust. Meetings, as well as other daily routines, are some of the key tools that supervisors use to ensure communication is happening on a regular and predictable schedule.

Good managers spend time thinking about and organizing their personal and team routines to ensure that their team members feel fully prepared and supported in doing their jobs well.

As you prepare to step into a supervisory role, thinking through your approach to meeting strategies and other key routines will help set yourself up for success.

Application Exercise

1. Routines are important for building trust with your team members. Are you good at establishing routines and following them? If not, how can you improve?

_____

_____

_____

_____

_____

_____

_____

_____

2. There will be times when you will need to have discussions with individuals on your team about their personal lives and personal problems. Are you comfortable with conversations like this and feel confident that you can support your employees? What skills might you need to learn about and develop?

_____

_____

_____

_____

_____

_____

_____

_____

_____

3. As a supervisor, you will be required to conduct meetings with your team regularly. Are you comfortable leading meetings? What skills do you need to improve in this area?

_____

_____

_____

_____

_____

_____

_____

_____

4. Starting early and staying late are two things a supervisor must be willing to do. Are you willing to spend more time at work in your new role? Why or why not?

_____

_____

_____

_____

_____

_____

_____

_____

CHAPTER 6

It's All in Your Head: Mental Pitfalls to Avoid

When I was very young, I always imagined being self-employed and leading a company of some kind. That dream became a reality much sooner than I had anticipated. At the age of 32, I was handed the reins of Monumental Sales, Inc.

However, when I did step into the leadership role, I wasn't as effective as I could have been. Upon receiving the promotion, I froze.

Why did I freeze? I had paralyzing feelings of self-doubt. I kept telling myself that people would realize that I didn't know what I was doing. I had convinced myself that I was not qualified and that I didn't have the experience necessary to lead an entire company.

I was afraid and felt like an imposter. All those feelings of self-doubt and inadequacy slowed me down, and I spent the first few months in the role not being as effective as I could have been.

I froze because I didn't want to make a mistake. So instead of making a mistake, I did nothing.

Chapter Overview

In this chapter, I will share with you some of the most common mental challenges or pitfalls which leaders tend to experience in new roles. Mental health and thinking patterns deserve a chapter in this book because they are critical to your success as a leader. No amount of skill or experience can make up for a negative or self-sabotaging mindset, so getting your mind right is necessary to excel as a manager, and it's something that isn't talked about nearly enough.

Key Points

Let's explore these common scenarios here, because accepting a new challenge and new role is likely always at least daunting or intimidating, and possibly even frightening. The fact is, you're going to feel a variety of emotions as you grow into your role as supervisor. I want you to remember that these emotional transitions or states are normal, and you can overcome them with time. Let's explore them one by one.

Imposter Syndrome

The most common challenge, and the one I experienced, is called Imposter Syndrome. This occurs when someone is given a position (usually due to being highly qualified) which drums up feelings of self-doubt and inadequacy. You suddenly fear you don't have the skills, knowledge, or qualifications to fill a supervisory role and this leaves you feeling like you're winging it or faking it, and that you're an imposter. Upon feeling unqualified to hold your position, you become afraid that others will find out you don't belong there, and you will fail.

You may also tend to compare yourself unfavorably to others. When you look at other supervisors, other leaders in your organization or other organizations, you might think, "Oh, my gosh, I can't accomplish that." But the fact of the matter is, you actually can.

Imposter Syndrome is very, very common, and you can overcome it by:

- Changing your self-talk. For example, instead of saying, "I can't do that" or "I don't have that capacity," try saying something like, "I can figure it out" or "I will learn how to do it."
- Stop comparing yourself to other, more experienced co-workers.
- Talk to others: your boss, peers, or a trusted family member with leadership experience.

You start by stepping out of your comfort zone and experiencing small successes. Learn to let positive recognition and feedback soothe your inner critic. You will make mistakes, and that's OK. However, the key to success is learning from those mistakes.

Paralysis by Analysis

The next syndrome or emotional state you may experience is "paralysis by analysis." This is the feeling of being overwhelmed with too much information, which leads to overthinking or overanalyzing every decision. This tendency is damaging because it bogs down the decision-making process, and your team will quickly become aware of this phenomenon.

When your team sees you second-guessing your judgment or when you make a decision and then say, "Oh, I'm not sure, I think we're going to do something a little bit different," that indecisiveness will bog down the decision-making process and grind your whole department to a halt. When you verbalize those second-guessed decisions, your co-workers and teammates will recognize your indecision and start questioning whether you are the right person for the role. Your team just wants you to make a decision – good, bad, or whatever – so that they can move forward. They want you to lead.

You need to recognize when you have fallen into the "paralysis by analysis" trap and call yourself out. I encourage you to ask your manager for help in recognizing the phenomenon as well. You can then start figuring out how to solve it. Start by educating yourself on ways of overcoming it. Please don't be afraid of reaching out to your counterparts and other people that you know in leadership roles.

Micromanagement Syndrome

The third syndrome or emotional state that you might experience is micromanagement. Micromanagement Syndrome is the tendency to closely monitor and control the work of your team members to ensure that everything is done in the right way. This practice will demotivate and damage the morale of your team members, who may start to wonder, "Why don't you just do it yourself?"

Micromanagers take the wind out of their workers' sails, and people just start to give up and take less pride in their work.

This very common emotional state is damaging to the supervisor and, ultimately, the department. Deep down, the micromanager doesn't believe that anyone can do the job better than himself or herself. But in reality, no one can do everything all the time. It's just impossible.

If you think you might have problems with this syndrome, realize that there are many ways to accomplish a task. Sometimes it may not be the route that you would take, but the fact of the matter is that there are different ways and different methods of accomplishing whatever needs to get done. So let your team members do their jobs their way, as long as it follows company policy and procedure and gets done on time. Give your team space to take ownership, and don't make them feel small.

And when it doesn't work out and takes longer or ends up not being the best practice, you can talk to your team members about it and help them understand other methods for completing work or projects. Help them understand and gain knowledge without ridicule or judgment.

Sometimes you have to let people make mistakes so that they can learn from their mistakes. Experience is the best teacher.

As a people-first supervisor, you need to let your reports make mistakes and coach them when appropriate, which will build respect and trust.

Superhero Syndrome

The fourth syndrome or emotional state that I want you to be aware of is called Superhero Syndrome. This syndrome represents a tendency to take on more responsibility and tasks than you can realistically handle. Supervisors develop this condition because, deep down, they don't trust their team members to get the job done.

Trust goes both ways. Once you gain the trust of your team members and they trust you, wonderful things happen. When that understanding is gained, you can concentrate on more important things, like reaching goals and growing a business.

Manifesting as the tendency to take on more responsibility and tasks than any one person can handle, Superhero Syndrome bogs down the organization, bogs down the department, and erodes the trust and confidence a team has in its leader. In addition, it can hamper the efficiency of an organization by blocking delegation that frees up a supervisor to concentrate on the larger issues.

Lone Wolf Syndrome

The fifth syndrome or emotional state is what I call Lone Wolf Syndrome. This is the practice of working independently and avoiding working with others or asking for help. When a supervisor uses this strategy, it may result in isolation and a lack of communication with his or her team and other members of the organization.

This syndrome is common because individuals believe they've been promoted because they can solve problems and come up with good answers. When they realize they don't have all the answers, rather than admitting it, they dig in and try to shelter themselves from others so they don't look stupid.

What's the solution? Don't isolate yourself from other people and think you'll figure this out over time. Instead, ask for help! People want to help other people succeed. Whether it is your team members, your manager, counterparts in your organization, friends, or family members, they all want you to succeed. Ask for help.

Inadequacy: Was I Born to Do This?

The sixth emotional state you may experience is a feeling of inadequacy which leads you to wonder, "What if I wasn't born with the skills to lead?"

Many people believe that you must be born with the skills necessary to be a leader or a supervisor. That's wrong.

I'm a firm believer that you can do anything you believe you can do. That means, if you're willing, you can learn to be a great leader. It won't happen overnight, and you're going to make mistakes. But do not think that in order to take on a supervisory role you need to have a silver tongue or be witty and extroverted. I'm not any of those. I'm an introvert, I am not witty, and I can never come back with a quick comment or zinger.

You don't have to be something you are not. Being a good supervisor is about building relationships with your team members and helping them be their best. It's not about being funny, cool, quick-witted, or good-looking. It's about being authentic and making each of your team members feel important.

You can be a great supervisor even if you prefer to be alone, even if you don't have any experience, even if you are the youngest person in the department, and even if you don't have a formal education.

I've seen it happen. The youngest person with the least experience and no formal management education can succeed in a supervisory role by being humble, considerate, compassionate, encouraging, a good trainer, and a good communicator.

You can do it! You can become a great supervisor simply by being a student of leadership and becoming a servant leader.

Overcoming These Syndromes

Now that you have some insight into what some of your emotional hurdles or challenges might be, you can recognize the traps, reach out to others, and find the resources and training to overcome them.

Bottom Line

The purpose of this book is to help you understand what you're walking into in a supervisory role. The emotional syndromes outlined above are very common. Successful supervisors learn how to overcome them by not getting bogged down with doubt and fear. Don't let them overwhelm you, because once you master these skills, the satisfying feelings of building a productive people-first culture can begin.

Application Exercise

1. Which of these syndromes or emotional states have you experienced before? How do you know? What was that experience like?

_____

_____

_____

_____

_____

_____

_____

_____

2. Which one of these syndromes or emotional states might you experience in your role as a supervisor? What can you do now to prepare yourself to be mentally strong in this situation?

_____

_____

_____

_____

_____

_____

_____

_____

_____

CHAPTER 7

Taking the Leap: Preparing for the Transition

Transitions can be scary. It seems that the bigger the transition, the scarier it is. Even small transitions can be scary. As I look back on my life (I'm now 65 years old), I realize that I've been through a lot of significant transitions.

Interestingly enough, I only remember the really good things and the really bad things, and other stuff is mostly forgotten. Some of the significant events that most of us experience are: getting our driver's license, high school graduation, marriage, college graduation, our first career job, the birth of our children, changing jobs, and promotions. I've been blessed with many joyful experiences, such as a rewarding career, a great marriage, world travel, raising wonderful and productive children, and spending time with our beautiful grandchildren.

Not all transitions are good; some are heartbreaking. In my case, I experienced the tragic death of our son, Simon, when he was only 33.

As the years pass, you will realize that life is not easy and that hard transitions are part of it. We can approach these challenges head-on or we can sidestep them. How we respond to these challenges has a profound impact on our ability to recover from hardships and step forward into opportunities.

Chapter Overview

Throughout my life, I have often chosen a road less traveled, which has been both exciting and discouraging. As a fellow leader and potential supervisor, you may have walked a similar path in life. For me, I've found that it's better to lean into my life and proactively live it rather than deal with the consequences of laziness or lack of focus. In that spirit, this chapter is dedicated to discussing what the leadership transition can look like and feel like, as well as some of the early steps you'll take in this transition. The more you know, the more you can prepare for it.

Key Points

Important Conversations: A Way to Ease the Transition

Whether you realize it or not, by picking up and reading this book you've already begun the emotional transition to something new. You're exploring whether or not moving into leadership or being a supervisor is in your future. Kudos to you for having the foresight to research your new endeavor.

As you prepare yourself to transition, I would encourage you to talk to some key people in your life about it. Start with your life partner – your husband, wife, or significant other. Explain what you're considering and why it's important to you to move into this leadership role. Share with them your dreams, hopes, and fears about taking this leap. Invite them to share theirs as well. I encourage you to listen with an open mind and a heart of compassion. This transition won't just impact you; it will impact all the people you love.

Once the two of you are on the same page with a decision, you can begin to explore the kind of support you'll need from them to be successful. Maybe you'll need a sounding board for your ideas, or maybe you'll just want someone with whom you can share your frustrations and victories at the end of a long day. Maybe you'll want advice as you move into this new role, and maybe you won't. Regardless, start to get a sense of what you (and your partner) will need to ensure this transition is well-supported, and commit to giving each other what you can.

Once you've talked with your significant other, you'll need to chat with your current supervisor about your plans. If you have a good boss who knows you well, wants you to succeed, and whom you trust, ask for their honest opinion of your plans. If you are ready for this journey, the conversation should be encouraging, exciting, and inspiring.

Do not, however, ask for anything from a boss who lacks confidence in you, does not know you well, whose opinion you do not respect, or who might perceive this news as a threat. Only inform her or him of your plans to pursue a supervisory role. This is done out of respect for the role or title, not the person.

A Working Timeline:
How Long Does This Transition Take?

The transition timeline depends on your situation. That said, assuming you are an outstanding performer in the eyes of your boss and plan to try to make the move within your current company, a six-month window is reasonable. This will allow you time to research, communicate, and train yourself to prepare for a successful transition.

However, if an opportunity arises tomorrow or next week, you can feel confident that you are ready and ahead of others who may be considering whether to apply for the role.

Simply by reading this book, you are going to understand what you're walking into and be more prepared than most. You already have more knowledge because you're doing your research and your homework.

What Should I Be Doing During the Transition?
What Baby Steps Can I Take Now?

The reflection exercises outlined in earlier chapters have given you a significant start in preparing yourself. That said, the transition period will give you a chance to fine-tune and revise your goals, values, and resume.

If you want to prepare yourself and get a leg up on the competition, I would encourage you to read a few books on "servant leadership." This will help you to begin to understand the importance of a people-first culture and philosophy.

As you work on these assignments, keep in mind that they are all working documents. They will evolve and change with your life experiences and maturity.

You can also use this time to begin to change your behaviors. Start paying attention to your vocabulary, use of language, physical appearance, and with whom and how you spend your time. Your time will start to become more and more valuable. It may be time to begin spending less time socializing with a co-worker who will most likely become your report.

I would sincerely encourage you to find and join a Toastmasters International Club. They're all over the world. It costs about $150 per year and represents a great investment that will significantly boost your confidence.

Toastmasters have self-directed pathways or leadership/educational modules that are included in your membership. You might consider enrolling in the "Dynamic Leadership" and "Leadership Development" modules. These two pathways will help you build your resume and move you toward becoming a great leader. To learn more, go to www.toastmasters.org. I joined Toastmasters at the age of 60; I wish I would have joined when I was 30!

Training Yourself:
How You Can Prepare for the Role

You can expect little or no training from your company. Very few companies have a leadership development program. That means it will be up to you to learn the skills necessary to be a great supervisor. Today, technology makes it a lot easier than it was 25 years ago.

Google, YouTube, and ChatGPT are some of my favorite resources. When you find an author or trainer you respect, subscribe to their posts, and you will be sent videos and information regularly.

These are some of the ways you can begin to educate yourself, and educating yourself is what you have to do. It's your responsibility; you can't rely on the company. If it's meant to be, it'll be up to you!

How Do I Shift My Relationships with My Co-Workers?

If you're aspiring to become a supervisor within the department in which you currently work, you're going to have to distance yourself from most co-workers. You can't be best friends with someone you're going to supervise.

Your reports and team members will pay attention to how much time and attention you give others. If you're giving individuals in your department a lot more attention and you're chatting with them, having lunch with them, or having a beer with them after work, others will notice. Your reports will perceive the time and attention as preferential treatment, which will reflect negatively on your performance.

So, if you are very close to any of your co-workers, begin to slowly back off and spend less and less time with them. A slow withdrawal can be done without alarming anyone or creating ill feelings.

When the time is right, you can share your intent and reasoning for the withdrawal. Hopefully, your relationship is strong and you will be able to re-engage with it when your circumstances change.

Bottom Line

Transitions are never easy. However, you can ease the growing pains of your transition into a supervisory role by preparing carefully. Communicating openly and appropriately with your family, current boss, colleagues, and others who play a role in your professional life will help ensure that your "tribe" is fully aware and will support you through your transition.

Application Exercise

1. For which parts of the transition discussed above do you feel prepared and ready? Why?

_____

_____

_____

_____

_____

_____

2. Which parts of the transition do you anticipate being most challenging for you? Why?

_____

_____

_____

_____

_____

_____

3. Who is in your support system? Who will you go to when things feel
   hard? Why?

_____

_____

_____

_____

_____

_____

_____

CHAPTER 8

Facing Your Fears:
Pushing through the 'What Ifs'

Fears of the Unknown Can Paralyze Those
Who Experience the Good Life

The term "good life" was introduced to me back in college. It was a description or definition of success. While each person likely has a different definition of what the good life looks and feels like, one thing is for sure: You won't get there if you aren't willing to name and face your fears.

No one ever succeeded by believing the voice in their head that said they weren't good enough. By allowing their fears to rule them, no one has ever succeeded. Thus, you too need to consider how you can push through your biggest fears to find success.

I truly hope your journey finds your own, special version of the good life.

Chapter Overview

To push through our biggest fears, you must first name them. Say them out loud. Give them space in your mind and heart. In so doing, you can begin to break them down and push past them. Many of our fears are born out of the unknown, the "what ifs." This chapter is all about naming some of the most common "what ifs" that are likely swirling through your mind. I will be giving you some ideas to help you begin working through those fears. Cheers to the journey! It is one worth taking.

Key Points

What If I Don't Have What It Takes to Be a Great Supervisor?

The short answer is that no one has EVERYTHING it takes, and many skills can be learned. That said, there are a few things that we've already discussed that will be helpful when acquiring the skills required for the role, which include:

- Improving your verbal and written communication skills – this includes writing, speaking, and general overall communication abilities
- Creating a people-first culture or a servant culture will assist you in helping your team members with their professional and personal struggles
- Increasing your organizational skills and prioritizing task management for you and your team
- Having a willingness to develop the skills needed to handle conflicts between team members
- Making a commitment to being a lifelong learner, curious about the way things work, and having a desire to make them better
- Being humble and teachable, admitting that you don't know all the answers, and being willing to learn from others
- Being open-minded, willing to listen to the ideas of others, and open to constructive feedback

If you are open to the ideas outlined above, your way of thinking is in line with what it takes to be successful as a supervisor.

What If I Feel Unsure About What Will Be Expected of Me in the Role?

Before applying for the role, it's important to understand the expectations. Doing so ensures that you know exactly what you're stepping into and that you have a clear set of responsibilities for which you will be evaluated. This can go a long way in setting you up for success in the role.

Ask for a job description and go through it carefully as you consider any new role. If a job description does not exist, which may be the case within many smaller companies, sit down with the person who would be your boss or the manager and ask questions about the position and expectations for the role.

Here are some questions I recommend asking when there is no job description:

1. What is the title of the role?
2. What is a brief overview of the position?
3. What are the duties and responsibilities of the role?
4. What qualifications are expected? Many times an educational component is a qualification. A company might request that an applicant has a high school diploma, two-year technical degree, four-year bachelor's degree, or master's degree.
5. Is experience considered within the realm of qualifications?
6. What skills and abilities are required?
7. Will I be expected to fill a production role as well as supervise? A "working supervisor" position is the expectation with many supervisory roles, but it's very important to understand that going in.
8. What is the salary, benefits, and other particulars of the compensation package? And any bonuses paid for exceeding expectations or meeting company targets?

Even if a job description does exist, not all of them are this thorough. In that case, use these questions to get answers to fill in the gaps in the existing description.

Now that you have a clear sense of the role, you can make an informed decision about whether or not you should move forward in the application process.

What If I Get the Job but End Up Hating It?
What If I Realize This Isn't for Me After All?

If this happens to you, don't panic! Initially, you may be overwhelmed with feelings of doubt and anxiety about what you need to learn and the challenges of the job. These feelings are not uncommon. Disliking the job early on isn't necessarily an indicator that you won't love it later. There is an acclimation period. Try to give it some time so you can gain some experience and confidence.

That said, if you still hate it after three, six, or even 12 months, you may want to consider your options. First, I'd recommend identifying exactly what it is about the role that you don't like. Maybe you could work with your manager to change those things and make the role more desirable and tenable. This is often easier than switching roles altogether.

If creating change within the role/organization isn't a possibility, I would encourage you to have a conversation with your boss, explaining your concerns and asking him or her, whether it is possible to return to your former position.

If you try all of these techniques and still decide you need to step out of the role, it's best to give your management team as much lead time as possible so that they can find a suitable replacement. Do not burn a bridge by resigning immediately!

Realizing that a supervisory role is not for you is not a failure. It's a movement toward your definition of success. You can now reassess your goals and desires and take the next step.

Bottom Line

It is normal to have fears and doubts when considering whether to leap into a supervisory role. Those fears are normal and confirm that you're engaged in the pros and cons of the transition.

Ultimately, great leaders don't let their fears stop them from realizing their fullest potential. The exercise below will help you think through some of your fears and push past them in pursuit of your goal.

Now that we've addressed some of your fears, it's time for you to continue your journey.

Application Exercise

1. In the past, how has your thinking or behavior kept you from succeeding? What fears do you commonly experience in a professional setting?

_____

_____

_____

_____

_____

_____

_____

_____

2. What current mental roadblocks will you need to get around? With which kind of thinking will you replace them?

_____

_____

_____

_____

_____

_____

_____

_____

3. How exactly will you do that?

_____

_____

_____

_____

_____

_____

_____

4. What kind of support will you need, and how will you go about
   getting it?

_____

_____

_____

_____

_____

_____

_____

CHAPTER 9

It's Decision Time:
Strategies for Making the Choice
That Is Right for You

Life is full of crossroads, moments when we stand at the intersection of choices, each path leading to a different destiny. These moments define us, shaping our future in profound ways. Remember those "Choose Your Own Adventure" books, in which if you wanted to ride a horse you turned to page 18, and if you wanted to climb a mountain you turned to page 28? It's now your very own "choose your own adventure" time or decision time, and the weight of choosing looms large.

Chapter Overview

And you've arrived. This is the very last chapter. You've done your reading, you've researched, you've journaled, you've reflected, and you've talked with people in your life. You've considered this from every angle, and your decision will be well-informed because of it. Congratulations on getting to this point. You will be rewarded for your thoughtfulness in one way or another, I promise!

This chapter is all about pushing past the paralysis of analysis (a very real thing) and providing you with some concrete tools to help you determine whether this is the right next step for you. The time has come. What are you going to do? What feels right? Let's review a bit of what we've discussed thus far and determine the likelihood of you succeeding in this supervisory or leadership role.

Key Points

Five Decision-Making Factors

As we wrap up, we will be focusing on five factors to assist you in making your decision.

1. Identifying your real motivation

When you completed your reflection activities, what did you learn about yourself? Are you motivated for the right reasons? As we discussed earlier, you must want it for the right reasons, and rewards – such as money or recognition – are *not* the right reasons.

They may be factors in your decision, but your primary purpose for transitioning into a supervisory role needs to be that you want to make a difference in the lives of other people. Do some real digging here and make sure this is what's truly driving you. If not, stop now.

2. Assessing the necessary skills

In your reflection activities, you assessed your current skill sets and asked yourself, "Do I have the drive to learn and improve the necessary skills needed to succeed in this role?" Some of the most important skills include public speaking, communication, holding others accountable, giving others direction, prioritizing, training, and problem solving.

You are not expected to have all the skills necessary when you begin your supervisory journey. The critical question is, do you have the drive to improve the skills you are lacking?

Are you willing to reach out to other people, join Toastmasters, take courses, read books, watch YouTube videos, listen to podcasts, and essentially do whatever it takes to develop those skills to become a successful supervisor? Be honest with yourself about the work involved in gaining the skills required. Not everyone will have the energy and motivation to do what is required. Hopefully, you do!

3. Learning from others

Are you willing to admit that you don't have all the answers? Are you willing to ask those who are more experienced for help and then actually take their advice when you believe it's valid?

If you think you have all the answers, it's very likely that you will not become a great leader. Humility is about being teachable. If you are teachable, you can improve. So be humble and curious, learn, and grow into a successful supervisor.

4. Evaluating company culture

I encourage you to examine the current culture of the company and ask yourself, "Does the culture of this organization match my vision of where I want to work?"

If the culture does not match your values, you are not going to be happy. The culture of any company is often a reflection (whether intentionally or subconsciously) of the person on top, i.e., the owner or president. If your values align with theirs, you are off to a good start. It will be your job to enhance the culture of your department by utilizing the existing foundation. However, if your values are not in line with those of the owner/president, it is time to look for a different company.

Are you willing to put in the time and energy to build a people-first culture in your department? The organizational culture and your departmental culture are very, very important to help you get the most out of your people and to succeed at a level that nobody has ever attained previously.

5. Aligning your personal and professional goals

Ask yourself, "Will this role move me toward fulfilling my long-term personal and professional goals?"

The role has to fulfill what you want to do – for yourself as an individual and for your family. They all have to mesh because when they don't mesh, you will be frustrated and your team and company will be frustrated. When people are frustrated, they don't do their best, and you and your team will not succeed at the levels you want. So take the time now and make sure your personal and professional goals line up with your goal of becoming a supervisor.

Are You Ready to Make the Decision?

There are all kinds of ways to make decisions. Some people use complicated decision-making matrices and some people simply throw darts at a wall. At the end of the day, I don't recommend either. You need to find that sweet spot where you can be thoughtful in your decision making without being crippled by the weight of the process.

In that spirit, the rest of this chapter focuses on an incredibly useful decision-making tool that will keep you focused on making a decision that is well thought out and aligns with your values and goals: the Ben Franklin Close approach.

This approach focuses on building a list of pros and cons for a specific choice or decision. The method allows you to better understand your values and priorities while also allowing you to explore the benefits of any given choice. In short, it is both an educational and an action-provoking tool.

Here is how the Ben Franklin Close method works:

- Take out a sheet of paper and make two columns. Label one column PROS and the other CONS.
- Brainstorm and list all the positive reasons (or pros) for moving in the direction of becoming a supervisor.
- Consider *all* of the relevant areas impacted by this decision: finances, family, goals, time, skills needed, etc.
- Next, write down all the negative reasons (or cons) for moving forward toward this position and write them out one by one.

- Again, make sure you address every aspect of your life that this choice will impact.
- Once you have brainstormed and written down everything, put your list down and step away from it. This brainstorming session is only your first draft. You need to take time to process and think about it.

Go back to this list a few times over the next week and add items. In addition, review your reflection exercises and pull any additional pros or cons from your notes. Continue to ponder the transition and write things down when they occur to you.

Over time, this list will grow and you will be able to look at it and use it to make a thoughtful, clear, and focused decision. Throughout the process, I encourage you to be honest with yourself. It can be easy to fool yourself into thinking that the pros outweigh the cons. In doing so, it would feel like you "won" the game – you accomplished your goal by determining that this was the right move for you.

But in reality, you "win" by coming to the RIGHT and HONEST conclusion about whether this is right for you. The point of this book was to help you make the best decision for you and your family.

Bottom Line

Decision making is not easy. It can be intimidating and overwhelming. The goal is to choose for the right reasons, with clarity and contentment.

It's now time for your decision. You are at a crossroads. What are you going to do?

Application Exercise

The Ben Franklin Close Decision-Making Process

PROS	CONS

My final decision:

_____

_____

_____

_____

_____

Key rationale:

_____

_____

_____

_____

_____

Next steps:

_____

_____

_____

_____

_____

Congratulations on reaching this milestone in your journey! Whether you've decided to step into a leadership role or have chosen to wait, your careful consideration speaks volumes about your dedication to personal growth and career clarity.

Embrace your choice confidently, knowing that you've taken the time to make the best decision for yourself and your family. Remember, this is just a step in your journey toward the "good life" and personal fulfillment. Keep moving forward with determination and enthusiasm – the best is yet to come.

www.ingramcontent.com/pod-product-compliance
Lightning Source LLC
Chambersburg PA
CBHW070852280326
41934CB00008B/1409